NORTHLAKE PUBLIC LIBRARY DISTRICT

3 1138 00189 9674

W9-BNT-901

DATE DUE

JA 1-9 '11			
AP 2 5 '12			

Demco, Inc. 38-293

CHE GUEVARA
The Making of a Revolutionary

❝*Above all, be sensitive, in the deepest areas of yourselves, to any injustices committed against whoever it may be anywhere in the world.* ❞ — Che Guevara

Life Portraits

CHE GUEVARA
The Making of a Revolutionary

By Samuel Willard Crompton

Gareth Stevens
Publishing

Please visit our web site at **www.garethstevens.com.**
For a free catalog describing Gareth Stevens Publishing's list of high-quality books,
call 1-800-542-2595 (USA) or 1-800-387-3178 (Canada).
Gareth Stevens Publishing's fax: 1-877-542-2596

Library of Congress Cataloging-in-Publication Data
Crompton, Samuel Willard.
　　Che Guevara: the making of a revolutionary / by Samuel Willard Crompton.
　　　　p. cm. — (Life portraits)
　　Includes bibliographical references and index.
　　ISBN-10: 1-4339-0053-X　　ISBN-13: 978-1-4339-0053-2 (lib. bdg.)
　　1. Guevara, Ernesto, 1928-1967—Juvenile literature. 2. Cuba—History—
1959–1990—Juvenile literature. 3. Latin America—History—1948–1980
Juvenile literature. 4. Guerrillas—Latin America—Biography—Juvenile literature.
I. Title.
　　F2849.22.G85C76　2009
　　980.03'5092—dc22
　　[B]　　　　　　　　　　　　　　　　　　　　　　　　　2008035444

This edition first published in 2009 by
Gareth Stevens Publishing
A Weekly Reader® Company
1 Reader's Digest Rd.
Pleasantville, NY 10570-7000 USA

Copyright © 2009 by Gareth Stevens, Inc.

Executive Managing Editor: Lisa M. Herrington
Creative Director: Lisa Donovan
Cover Designer: Keith Plechaty
Interior Designers: Yin Ling Wong and Keith Plechaty
Publisher: Keith Garton

Produced by Spooky Cheetah Press
www.spookycheetah.com
Editor: Stephanie Fitzgerald
Designer: Kimberly Shake
Cartographer: XNR Productions, Inc.
Proofreader: Jessica Cohn
Indexer: Madge Walls, All Sky Indexing

All rights reserved. No part of this book may be reproduced, stored in a retrieval
system, or transmitted in any form or by any means, electronic, mechanical,
photocopying, recording, or otherwise, without the prior written permission of the
copyright holder. For permission, contact **permissions@gspub.com.**

Printed in the United States of America

1 2 3 4 5 6 7 8 9 12 11 10 09 08

TABLE OF CONTENTS

NORTHLAKE PUBLIC LIBRARY DIST.
231 N. WOLF ROAD
NORTHLAKE, IL 60164

In December 1964, Che Guevara traveled to New York City to address the General Assembly of the United Nations on behalf of Cuba.

CHAPTER ONE

A MESSAGE TO THE WORLD

KABOOM! ON DECEMBER 11, 1964, THE SOUND of a bazooka blast echoed through the halls of the United Nations (U.N.) building in New York City. No one was hurt. The building wasn't damaged. Everyone inside the building and on the street below heard the deafening sound, though. This was the most violent attack ever to have occurred at the United Nations. The target was Ernesto "Che" Guevara. He was visiting the U.N. as a representative of the Cuban government. Amazingly, Che didn't even pause in his speech to acknowledge the sound of the explosion.

Che stood in front of the General Assembly of the U.N. dressed in olive-green fatigues and army boots. All that was missing was his trademark black beret. It was no accident that Che wore an army uniform instead of a suit for his visit to the United Nations. He had accomplished many things in his life. He had practiced medicine, fought in wars, even held government positions. The 36-year-old was technically a doctor and a diplomat, yet he was, first and foremost, a revolutionary.

In 1959, Che had fought alongside Fidel Castro in the Cuban Revolution. They had worked to overthrow the government of Fulgencio Batista. They had fought to give the poor people of Cuba a better life. On the day of the bazooka attack, Che was at the U.N. to argue for the rights of poor and oppressed people around the world. He was there to criticize the powerful nations of the world—such as the United States—that he felt kept poorer countries down. He was there, he said, to fight for change.

The Cuban Revolution

Fulgencio Batista (1901–1973) was a military leader who seized power in Cuba in 1952. Under his rule, Cubans had few rights. Government officials and the upper class got rich through agreements with foreign companies, but the common people lived in poverty. Anyone who spoke out against the government met a violent end. Fidel Castro attempted to overthrow the government in 1953, but failed. In December 1956, Castro's group of revolutionaries, which included Che Guevara, embarked on a successful campaign to rid Cuba of Batista. Castro might have had good intentions when he started the revolution. After he seized power, however, he also became a dictator.

THE MESSAGE

An important part of Che's speech that day was the idea of peaceful coexistence. He believed that rich, capitalist nations such as the United States and Great Britain did not want to live in peace with poor Third World nations. The Third World included nations such as Cuba and many countries in Africa. Che believed that capitalist nations just wanted to use poor countries for their own economic gain. For hundreds of years, powerful nations established colonies in poor areas of the world. These governments then got rich by exploiting the Third World countries' abundant natural resources—such as sugar, spices, or precious minerals. The native inhabitants didn't see any gain from these arrangements, though. In fact, they often lived in poverty and were mistreated by the government.

> **"We want to build a better life for our people."**
> – CHE GUEVARA

According to Che, the world could be divided into two camps: socialist and capitalist. He had a very strict and narrow definition for each. Che felt that the capitalists were rich countries that took advantage of others. Socialists wanted to live in equality—with each other and the rest of the world. Che felt capitalist governments would never let that happen, though. "We want to build socialism," he said. "We have declared that we are supporters of those who strive for peace. ... We want to build a better life for our people." A few minutes later, he finished his speech with the rallying cry of the Cuban Revolution, "Patria o muerte!" (Fatherland or death!)

Capitalism vs. Socialism

The word *socialism* is based on the word *society*. In this political and economic system, the needs and desires of society as a whole are supposed to be more important than those of the individual. Under socialism there is no such thing as private property. The government mainly controls the businesses and factories that produce goods. In a capitalist society, a country's economy is organized so that businesses and factories belong to individuals rather than to the government.

AN UNLIKELY HERO

As Che finished his speech, New York City police tried to figure out where the bazooka blast had come from. They found the weapon hidden among some low brush across the East River from the U.N. building. Several Cuban exiles were found and arrested. After the speech, journalists pressed Che for a comment on the attack. *The New York Times* described his reply: "He said, with a languid wave of his cigar, that the explosion 'has given the whole thing more flavor.'" The comment was typical of Che. He was never one to show fear.

Che's visit to New York was a triumph for his cause. This is surprising considering how vocal he was about his hatred for the United States and everything for which the U.S. government stood. For many people, however, Che was a hero. He was a person who believed in equality for all people. He was someone who was willing to fight—and die—to bring freedom and quality of life to others.

By the time he died at 39 years old, Che had become an icon. He was both hated and held apart. Almost 40 years after Che's death, *Time* magazine compiled a special issue on the 100 most influential persons of the twentieth century. Ernesto "Che" Guevara made that list. The violent revolutionary who believed in the overthrow of capitalist governments was listed under "Heroes & Icons." ❖

In 1997, thousands of Cubans lined up to pay their respects to their fallen hero. Che's remains had recently been returned to Cuba, and his coffin was on display in Havana at the Plaza of the Revolution.

Che was the firstborn of Ernesto Sr. and Celia, and was always his parents' favorite. Che and his mother were especially close throughout his life.

CHAPTER TWO

EARLY BATTLES

ERNESTO "CHE" GUEVARA DE LA SERNA WAS BORN in Rosario, Argentina, on May 14, 1928. For most of his life, he celebrated his birthday on June 14, 1928, though. In fact, some people continue to recognize this as his birthday. The little boy's parents, Ernesto Guevara Lynch and Celia de la Serna, deceived Che—and everyone else. The couple got married just seven months before Che was born. They did not want their families to know that Celia was already pregnant at the time of the wedding.

Che's parents came from the Argentine upper class. His mother had royalty in her family tree. His father's family had been among Argentina's wealthiest families. Most of the money had disappeared by the time Che was born, however. It was mostly lost through bad business investments and high living by some family members.

From the time he was little, Che showed natural leadership abilities. He had a way of making everyone around him feel important.

The Guevaras didn't have much when Che was growing up. That didn't matter, though. Che's parents didn't care about money at all. They were more interested in people, especially unusual ones, books, especially radical ones, and ideas. Che inherited his parents' lack of interest in material wealth. Material things were of little or no importance to them.

Che was the eldest of five children. He was 18 months old when his sister Celia was born. She was followed by a brother,

Roberto, in 1932 and another sister, Ana Maria, in 1934. Che's youngest brother, Juan Martín, was born in 1943.

The Guevara household was often chaotic. There were no set mealtimes. The children just ate when they were hungry. There were always tools, bicycles, and lots of books spread all over the house. The Guevaras' home was often filled with visitors as well. "[Che], as usual, was the center of all the gatherings," his father later recalled.

Che was also the boss of his younger siblings. He was his parents' favorite and had plenty of energy. Although Che seemed destined for leadership from the time he was a child, he also had a kind and loyal nature. "With his traditional loyalty he never dropped any of his friends in favor of those from a better social background," his father said. "He always had the capacity to bond with the heterogeneous [varied] group who surrounded him, without ever making anyone feel overpowered by his presence."

Some people who visited the family home thought it a shame so much attention went to Che. His parents made no secret of the fact that they thought Che was special. Those who knew the family well, however, realized that the little boy was special in more ways than one. Yes, he was his parents' favorite; yes, he received the most attention. He also had the hardest path of anyone in the family—he had an incurable disease.

> "[Che] always had the ability to bond with the ... group who surrounded him without ever making anyone feel overpowered by his presence."
>
> – ERNESTO GUEVARA, CHE'S FATHER

OVERCOMING OBSTACLES

The Guevara clan was happy and healthy for the most part. Che's mother had a host of allergies and a slight touch of asthma. But nothing in the family background prepared Che's parents for his sudden battles with asthma.

When Che was 2 years old, his mother took him swimming. Soon after, the little boy had his first serious asthma attack. For years, Che's father blamed his wife for their son's ailment. Asthma ran in the family, though—it was likely Che would suffer from it. His swim that day had nothing to do with the problem. Unfortunately for little Che, what had been a rather lucky, even charmed, life now became one of constant challenge and struggle. Years later, his father described Che's condition:

> [Che] had scarcely begun to talk when he learned to say, 'Daddy, injection,' whenever his asthma got the better of him. This gives an idea of his suffering; children on the whole are scared of needles, but he had realized that it was the only thing that helped him when he had an attack. Anybody with any sensitivity who has to witness daily the suffering of a child from an illness that, although not fatal, is chronic, must be affected. I never got used to the sound of his breathing—a noise not unlike a cat's purring.

Che's parents tried all sorts of doctors, hospitals, and remedies to help with his asthma. The only thing that gave the boy some relief was a move to the higher, drier climate of the mountainous province of Cordoba, in central Argentina. When Che was

*Che (second from right) never let his asthma keep him from having
fun. He loved to play with his cousins and siblings, and was always the
first to try something exciting or dangerous.*

5 years old, the family settled in the small city of Alta Gracia.
They lived there for 10 years.

Che was very studious from a young age and loved to read.
He had other hobbies, as well. His father explained:

> *His natural inclination [was] to study and read ... and
> he always found time to be on his own, to concentrate
> on his books. He had a rare quality that was a trait of*

his personality: an enjoyment of reading and studying, to which he devoted a lot of time; but these did not prevent him from practicing sports, or from playing chess as he always had, or from meeting up with his friends or going on outings and excursions.

Some people might have used their asthma as an excuse to hide from the world. It was not in Che's nature to give in to adversity, though. Instead of hiding behind his illness, Che became something of a daredevil. He ate chalk in school, walked on logs over dangerous ravines, and was almost always the first person to volunteer to do a dangerous thing.

Che also loved to play soccer. He was determined to live normally, just like other boys. Che played just as hard—or harder—than his teammates. A friend on the sidelines always

The Pig

Che found some of his best friends for life on the soccer field. He was especially close to the Granado family. One of the Granado boys was Che's age. Another, Alberto, was about seven years older. Alberto gave Che one of his first nicknames. He called him "Chancho," which means "the pig." Young Che was not a fan of bathing. He would often go weeks without washing his soccer shirt. He would even brag about it!

The Spanish Civil War

Spain had been a monarchy. Then, in 1931, a revolution created the new Spanish Republic. Five years later, General Francisco Franco started the Spanish Civil War (1936–1939). It has often been referred to as the dress rehearsal for World War II (1939–1945). Bombing from the air was done for the first time, and the savage fighting claimed the lives of about one million Spaniards. When the fighting ended in March 1939, Franco created a one-man dictatorship.

had his inhaler at the ready. Many times his parents were called to a soccer or rugby match, where they'd find their son doubled over in obvious pain. There were frequent trips to doctors, but nothing like a cure.

TAKING SIDES

In addition to his other pursuits, Che also showed an early interest in politics and warfare. In 1936, the Spanish Civil War broke out. Both of Che's parents had Spanish ancestry, so the entire family took a great interest in the war. Che started playing chess around this time. He often arranged chess pieces on maps and boards to follow the progress of the war. He would even act out important battles with his chess pieces and his friends. Much to his sorrow, and to his father's too, Spain was in the hands of a dictator by the summer of 1939.

The Young Operative

Che got his first taste of espionage during World War II, when the officers of a Nazi warship hid from British cruisers in an Argentine bay. Che and his father used binoculars to spy on the German ship. They pretended to be government agents, making sure the Germans did not spread propaganda among the Argentine people.

Before long, though, there would be another war to capture their attention. When World War II began, father and son both rooted for the Allies against the Germans and Italians. They were disappointed when Argentina declared neutrality. They wanted their country to fight with the Allied Powers, such as the United States, Britain, and the Soviet Union—not sit on the sidelines. Argentina didn't enter the war until 1945, when it was certain that the Allied Powers would defeat the Nazis. At that point, Che was almost finished with high school and looking forward to his future. For the moment, however, it was uncertain what that future would hold.

A NEW DIRECTION

After he graduated from high school, Che planned to enter the University of Buenos Aires. He was going to study engineering. Then something happened that spring that changed the direction of his life.

By the time Che (first row, second from left) graduated from high school, his personality was set. He was a curious combination of bookworm and daredevil.

In May 1947, Che learned that his beloved grandmother, Ana Isabel, was seriously ill. He rushed to her home in Buenos Aires. For 17 days Che stayed by his grandmother's side and took care of her. Che had always been close with his grandmother and his paternal aunt Beatriz. Even so, family members were astonished at the change that came over him when he tended to his grandmother. It was as if he was a different person. When she died, Che was devastated. He no longer thought about studying engineering. He was determined to become a doctor. ❖

Che loved to travel and meet new people. He took his first big road trip on a bicycle with a motor attached.

CHAPTER THREE

ON THE ROAD

C HE BEGAN HIS MEDICAL STUDIES AT THE University of Buenos Aires in 1947. He had always been a good student. He had gotten by rather easily during his elementary and high school years. Now, for the first time, Che had to work very hard to do well in school.

Che had always been interested in allergies. He saw how his mother suffered from her allergies, and he felt they might be the root of his asthma. When he started medical school it was with dreams of becoming a famous researcher.

Che was 18 when he began his medical studies, and he had grown into a handsome young man. It seemed as if he had a new girlfriend every week or so. None of these relationships were serious, though. Che was just looking to have fun. Somehow he managed to get good grades and enjoy life at the same time. One of his favorite pastimes was traveling.

Migrant workers pick much of the produce grown in the United States. If not for this cheap labor, food prices would be much higher.

LEGENDARY ROAD TRIP

Che's family had traveled a bit when he was growing up. Now that he was a young man, the world was wide open to him. Che was ready to hit the road. First he hitchhiked through southern Argentina. Then he planned a more ambitious trip. On January 1, 1950, Che left home, riding a bicycle he had equipped with a small motor. The motor wasn't powerful enough for the bike, though. Che had to pedal his way up some of the countryside's larger hills.

The first few days of Che's trip covered areas that he knew well. Within a week he was far from anything with which he was familiar. As he traveled, Che began meeting and befriending locals. Some of the people found him rather strange. On one occasion, Che met a migrant worker. This man didn't travel just for the fun of it. He traveled to find work and make money. The man found Che's reasons for traveling hard to understand. Che later recalled their meeting:

> [The worker] was coming from the cotton harvest in Chaco and thought that, after doing nothing for a while, he would go to San Juan, to the grape harvest. When he found out that I planned to tour several provinces and that my motive was purely for the experience, he grabbed his head with both hands and said in desperation: "Mamma mia, all that effort for nothing?"

Migrant Workers

Migrant work has a long tradition in both North and South America. Migrant workers are people who move from place to place with the seasons in search of agricultural work. They may pick corn in the north, tobacco in the south, and grapes in between. In the 1950s, when Che traveled, South America had more migrant workers than North America. Starting in the 1960s, the United States became the destination for millions of migrant workers. Today, more produce is picked by migrant workers from other countries than by United States citizens.

The migrant worker allowed Che to tag along with him. He introduced the young traveler to many other people. When Che returned to Buenos Aires after three months on the road, he was a changed person. He had always enjoyed meeting people from different social classes, but this trip was different. Che had seen more of the poor workers who lived in his country.

Che returned to his medical studies, but he had found a new attraction: the open road. Within a year, he was planning his next big trip.

HEADS AND TAILS

One of Che's oldest friends was Alberto Granado. Alberto, who was seven years older than Che, was already a doctor. From the time they were children, the friends dreamed of taking a road trip together. In the winter of 1952, they were ready for the biggest trip of their lives. The two set off in January 1952 aboard a motorcycle Alberto called *La Poderosa II,* meaning "the powerful one." This wasn't a very fitting name, though. The motorcycle broke down about a third of the way into their trip. For the rest of the journey, they mostly hitchhiked.

At the start of the trip, Che explained his political philosophy to his friend, whom he called Petiso. He said:

> *Petiso, this is how it is. Heads and tails, always the two sides of the coin. The beauty of the landscape and the natural wealth of the land set against the poverty of those who work it. The nobility and generosity of the poor set against the mean and sordid spirits of the landowners and of those who rule the country.*

A visit to Chile's Chuquicamata copper mine raised serious questions in the minds of Che and Alberto. Che became convinced that violent revolution was the only way to change South America's unequal social structure.

"Heads and tails" became an expression used by the two whenever they saw something strange or unjust. It became the guiding motto of their trip. And what a trip it was! For five months the friends traveled through parts of Bolivia, Peru, Ecuador, Brazil, and Colombia. They visited the ancient ruins of Machu Picchu and walked through the great cities of Lima, Cuzco, and Caracas. If one event came to symbolize the journey, however, it was their visit to the mine at Chuquicamata, Chile.

The copper mine was the largest of its kind in the world. Che and Alberto were anxious to see it. They knew the American-owned mine was hugely profitable. They just didn't know how poorly paid the miners were. They would soon find out that the laborers made less than a dollar a day. Alberto and Che reached the mine in the late afternoon and set up camp for the night. They met a middle-aged couple who had nowhere to go and were living on the street. This type of rough living was not unusual for Alberto and Che. But the husband and wife weren't living this way by choice. The husband had been fired from his mining job because the owners knew he was a communist. (Communism is a system of government in which a single authoritarian party controls the means of production and, in theory, economic goods are distributed equally among the people.)

The couple had left their children with friends while they tried to find work. They could not find jobs at Chuquicamata, so they were headed for more remote areas. They thought mine owners at smaller mines would not care about their workers' beliefs.

Che and Alberto were stunned both by the couple's poverty and by the courage they displayed. As they talked, Che learned that the couple had no money, no possessions, and nowhere to sleep. He later described the scene in his journal:

> *The couple, numb with cold, huddling together against each other in the desert night, were a living representation of the proletariat [working class] in any part of the world. They had not one single miserable blanket to cover themselves with, so we gave them one of ours and Alberto and I wrapped the other around us as best we could. It was one of the coldest times in my life, but also one which made me feel a little more brotherly toward this strange, for me at least, human species.*

The next day, Che and Alberto made it to the copper mine by afternoon. They couldn't believe how much earth had been moved—and how much copper had been recovered. They were even more shocked by the way the workers were treated. The workers were preparing to strike, all because the owners would not increase wages by a dollar a day. Meanwhile, the mine was producing material valued at $1 million dollars a day.

It is difficult to say just when Che started to believe in violent revolution to overthrow the capitalist system. Meeting the communist couple that night and seeing the exploitation of the mine workers the next day likely marked a real turning point.

The Motorcycle Diaries

Che's notebooks from his 1952 trip with Alberto Granado later became a book called *The Motorcycle Diaries*. In 2004, the book was made into a movie starring a young Mexican actor named Gael García Bernal as Che. The movie's motto was "Let the world change you … and you can change the world." Alberto, who was in his 80s at the time, served as a special consultant to the film. He accompanied the actors on the shoot and advised them about what it had been like to ride a motorcycle through South America. Critics and moviegoers alike saluted *The Motorcycle Diaries* as one of the best films of 2004.

A few weeks later, the duo headed for the magnificent ruins at Machu Picchu in Peru. As they approached the site, Che and Alberto were befriended by a local hotel owner. The man offered to put them up for free because the tourist business was slow.

As Che and Alberto spent the better part of a day touring the ruins, they talked about how great South American culture had been before the appearance of the Spanish conquistadors. The Incas of Peru had created a thriving civilization that was destroyed by European invaders.

> "Revolution without firing a shot? You're crazy, Petiso."
>
> – CHE GUEVARA

Surely Che and Alberto found that thought incredibly frustrating. In fact, Alberto was moved to suggest starting a revolution. He wanted to restore the glory of ancient Peru by bringing an Indian politician to power. "I'll form a pro-Indian party," he said. "I'll take all these people to the coast to vote, and that'll be the start of the new Tupac Amaru revolution, the American Indian revolution!"

Alberto expected to hear praise for his idea. Surely Che would be all for giving power back to the poor indigenous people of South America. Instead he received a surprising answer. "Revolution without firing a shot?" Che said. "You're crazy, Petiso."

When Che and Alberto returned to the hotel, they found themselves without rooms. When paying customers checked in, the hotel owner threw his freeloading customers out. The tourists who took their rooms were Americans. In his journal, Che vented his anger toward the "blonde, camera-toting, sport-shirted correspondents from another world."

Machu Picchu

Machu Picchu is located high in the mountains of Peru. It is often called "The Lost City of the Incas." The Incas built the structures there around 1450. The Incas ruled one of the largest empires in South America from about 1200 to the mid-1500s. Machu Picchu covers just 5 square miles (13 square kilometers), but it houses a completely self-contained city. There are enough agricultural terraces to have fed the city inhabitants, as well as abundant natural springs. Machu Picchu also includes about 150 homes, as well as palaces, temples, baths, and storage rooms. The city was abandoned in the mid-1500s, not long after Spanish conquistadors arrived. The Inca Empire ultimately collapsed under Spanish rule.

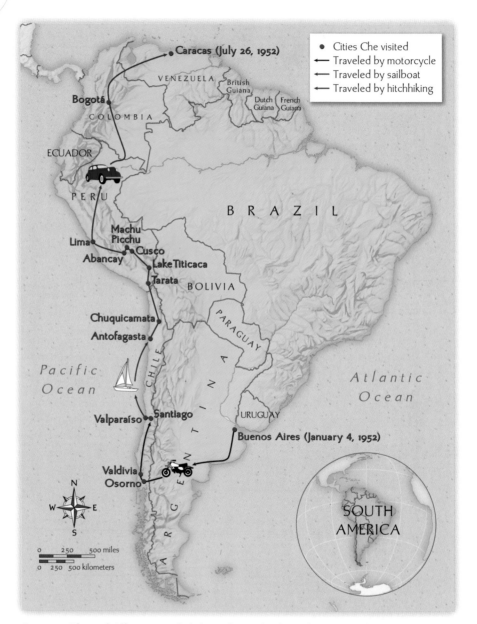

In 1952, Che and Alberto traveled through much of South America during the almost seven months they spent on the road. It was a life-changing experience for both of them. Che wrote a book about the journey that was later made into a movie.

Hansen's Disease

Hansen's disease, once known as leprosy, is an infectious disease that spreads through the body and causes the skin to have a mottled, decaying look. For many years, sufferers were discriminated against. They were shunned by society and hidden away far from the sight of "normal" people. Che's treatment of the afflicted in Peru showed the parts of his nature that led him to become a freedom fighter.

HOMEWARD BOUND

Alberto and Che traveled through Peru and spent three weeks at a leper colony near the Amazon River. Alberto had already studied the skin disease, which would come to be known as Hansen's disease. He informed Che about the dangers of working with people who had it. Once they arrived at the colony, neither man showed any fear of contracting the disease, however. They played soccer with the patients, had parties thrown for them, and generally had a good time. For Che, it was yet another revelation about the cruelties of society. Once again he saw how a group of people could be pushed into the margins.

The two friends parted in Colombia. Alberto stayed there to study with another specialist in Hansen's disease. Che traveled to Caracas, Venezuela, and then boarded a plane for Miami, Florida. By the late summer of 1952, he was back in Buenos Aires preparing for his final year of medical school. ❖

NORTHLAKE PUBLIC LIBRARY DIST.
231 N. WOLF ROAD
NORTHLAKE, IL 60164

Raúl Castro (left) and Che (right) did not have much in common personally, but they shared an undying belief in revolution.

CHAPTER FOUR

SETTING A NEW COURSE

IN THE SPRING OF 1953, CHE CALLED HIS FATHER with some very exciting news. He was a doctor! Che's parents couldn't have been more proud. If they thought their beloved son was about to settle down, however, they were mistaken. Two months after earning his degree, Che was on the road again.

After traveling through Ecuador and Chile, Che decided to move on to Guatemala, a nation in Central America. Guatemala was very different from Che's home country of Argentina—or any other place he had seen. The scenery was not what drew him north in such a hurry, however. In 1953, Guatemala was in the middle of a great economic experiment.

Two years earlier, Jacobo Arbenz had been elected president. Under his direction, in 1953, Guatemala became the first Central American country to nationalize the property of a large

American company. President Arbenz took land that was owned by the United Fruit Company and planned to return it to the Guatemalan peasants.

BITTER FRUIT

The United Fruit Company, based in Boston, Massachusetts, had a large presence in Guatemala. In fact, the company was said to be as powerful as the Guatemalan government itself. The company, which exported bananas, owned about a quarter of all Guatemalan land. That was more land than was owned by

Banana Republic

People in the United States had never tasted bananas until around 1870. That's when the fruit was first introduced in North America. Once they tasted bananas, Americans quickly agreed that it was one of nature's perfect foods. The United Fruit Company proceeded to make millions of dollars importing bananas from Guatemala and other Central American countries to the United States. These countries became known as "banana republics." The expression refers to Central American and South American states that had little to export, and little to sell, other than bananas. Today the expression *banana republic* is used to describe any country that has become too dependent on one crop for its survival.

The United Fruit Company dominated Guatemala between 1920 and 1953. During that time, United Fruit was the single biggest landowner in the entire country.

all of the common people put together. United Fruit also controlled the only railway to the sea. This meant the United Fruit Company could quickly and easily export its products to the United States and other countries. All this changed in 1953, when the Guatemalan government took about one-half of all the United Fruit Company's land and proposed to distribute it among the Guatemalan peasants.

When Che reached Guatemala, he was excited by the changes he saw there. He admired President Arbenz's plans to make life better for the poorest in his country. He showed his hatred for the

United Fruit Company—the face of America in Guatemala—in a letter to his beloved Aunt Beatriz. He wrote in part:

> Along the way I have had the opportunity to pass through the dominions of United Fruit, convincing me once again of just how terrible these capitalist octopuses are. I have sworn ... that I won't rest until I see these capitalist octopuses annihilated. In Guatemala I will perfect myself and achieve what I need to be an authentic revolutionary.

MAKING CONNECTIONS

Che was busy following politics in Guatemala, but he managed to find time for personal relationships. He made many friends and even had romantic relationships. Che liked women of all types, but he had a chauvinistic attitude toward them. He shared his feelings and dreams with women. He talked about his ideas and goals only with men. He felt that most women were not adventurous enough for him. That thinking changed when he met Hilda Gadea.

Che and Hilda were friends at first. But he was increasingly attracted to her bright and open mind. Before long, the two were romantically involved and living together. Visitors complained that the apartment was completely taken over by books and that there was no place to sit. This was the kind of Bohemian lifestyle that Che had grown up with. Hilda fit into it perfectly.

During his first winter in Guatemala, Hilda introduced Che to a group of Cubans. The men had been exiled from their country

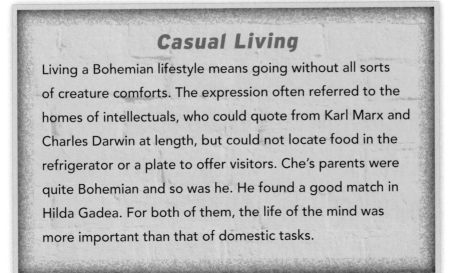

Casual Living

Living a Bohemian lifestyle means going without all sorts of creature comforts. The expression often referred to the homes of intellectuals, who could quote from Karl Marx and Charles Darwin at length, but could not locate food in the refrigerator or a plate to offer visitors. Che's parents were quite Bohemian and so was he. He found a good match in Hilda Gadea. For both of them, the life of the mind was more important than that of domestic tasks.

for attempting a revolution. They were intent on returning to Cuba to try again. What none of them realized was that a revolution was brewing right there in Guatemala.

THE END OF THE EXPERIMENT

The United States government was alarmed by what was happening in Guatemala. President Dwight D. Eisenhower saw Arbenz's move to nationalize the land as a move toward socialism. He also had an interest in keeping the lands under the control of United Fruit, an American company.

In June 1954, Guatemala City was attacked by planes built in the United States. Whether Americans flew them is uncertain. At the same time, a United States–trained army of Guatemalan exiles began crossing the border from Honduras. They were going to overthrow the government and oust Arbenz from power.

The Guatemalan coup of 1954 was planned in Washington, D.C., but carried out by right-wing Guatemalans. They were delighted to get rid of their new president and squash his plans for distributing the land to peasants.

Che and many of his friends welcomed the start of violence. They believed President Arbenz, a former army colonel, would stand firm and fight the returning exiles. They were cruelly disappointed when Arbenz resigned from office and went into exile, leaving the socialist experiment in shambles and the Guatemalan military in control. Che vented about the turn of events in a letter to his mother. He wrote:

> *The Americans have totally dropped the good-guy mask that [Franklin] Roosevelt had given them and they are committing an outrage and a half around here. If matters reach a point where it is necessary to fight against planes*

and modern troops sent by the fruit company or the USA, there will be a fight. The morale of the people is very good and the shamefaced attacks, added to the lies of the international press, have united all those who were indifferent towards the government and there is a really combative mood.

Che did not participate in the fighting, but he was not a citizen of Guatemala. When the battle ended, he had to look for a safe place to stay. He found refuge in the Argentine embassy in Guatemala City. Hilda, meanwhile, had gone to the Peruvian embassy. Che spent almost four months in the embassy. He could

Following the coup, Jacobo Arbenz (second from left) — the legally elected president — was forced to leave the country.

have left the country sooner if he had been willing to go home to Argentina, but he refused. His experiences—both on the road and in Guatemala—had turned Che into a radical. He intended to be a revolutionary. When he left Guatemala, it would be to go to someplace where he might help institute change.

THE 26TH OF JULY MOVEMENT

In the fall of 1954, Che left for Mexico. Mexico City was home to many artists and radical thinkers. In fact, it was perhaps the most radical of all South American capital cities at the time.

Hilda moved to Mexico, too. By the spring of 1955, she and Che were back together again. Hilda was completely in love with him, but Che still thought of Hilda as a friend. He wasn't in love with her.

In the summer of 1955, Hilda introduced Che to another group of Cubans who would change his life forever. The men were Cuban exiles led by Raúl Castro, the younger brother of Fidel. The Castro brothers had attempted to overthrow the Cuban government two years earlier. Now, the exiles were regrouping in Mexico and planning to attempt another coup. They called their group of revolutionaries the 26th of July Movement.

In July 1953, Fidel Castro, his brother Raúl, and about 200 other Cubans attempted a coup. When it failed, both Castro

> "[Che] was one of those people that everyone immediately cares about—it was his naturalness, his simplicity, his sense of comradeship and all his virtues."
>
> – FIDEL CASTRO

Latin America: Land of Military Coups

A coup (which means "strike" or "blow" in French) refers to the overthrow of a government. Latin American countries have been especially vulnerable to coups over the past 100 years. Part of the reason is that many Latin American governments tend to be very dependent on the military to keep them in power. Many South American leaders have come to power through the support of the military. They've stayed in office for many years, only to be removed later by that same military.

brothers were sent to prison. Though each was given a long sentence, the Cuban dictator, Fulgencio Batista, allowed them to be freed after just two years. When they were released, both men were exiled. Raúl arrived in Mexico in the spring of 1955. Fidel followed that summer. Soon after his brother arrived in Mexico, Raúl introduced Fidel to Che.

The two met in the evening and talked together until dawn. By the time the sun came up, Che had signed on as a member of the 26th of July Movement to overthrow Batista's government in Cuba. "[Che] had a gift for people," Fidel remembered years later. "He was one of those people that everyone immediately cares about—it was his naturalness, his simplicity, his sense of comradeship, and all his virtues." ❖

A YOUNG FAMILY MAN

Che's daughter Hildita was born in February 1956. From the beginning, Che was a devoted father. He spent hours just watching his daughter, whom he called his "little Mao." When he wrote to his mother, he said:

> I am very happy with her, my Communist soul swells with pride as she is identical to Mao [Zedong]. Even now the bald patch in the middle of her head can be seen, the kind eyes of the leader and his protruding double chin; for the time being she weighs less than the leader, since she barely surpasses five kilos, but with time she will catch up. She is more spoilt than the majority of children and she eats like I used to eat.

Che liked being a father, but he was not much of a husband. He had mixed feelings about Hilda. When he realized that her ideals were much less radical than his, his feelings for Hilda diminished even more. Hilda believed in moderate, economic change, such as Jacobo Arbenz had attempted in Guatemala. Che, on the other hand, was convinced that violent revolution was the only way to make a better world.

Despite his dedication to the 26th of July Movement, some of the Cuban exiles did not like having an Argentine in their midst. Over time, the intensity of his commitment won their respect. He battled his asthma as much as ever, but he would not let it stop him. To prepare for the physical aspect of war, he even tried to climb Mexico's highest mountain, the volcanic Mount Popocatépetl. Both times he had to stop shy of the summit.

Chairman Mao

Mao Zedong was born in China in 1893. The communist leader founded the People's Republic of China in 1949 and ruled it until his death in 1976. When Mao was born, China was ruled by an emperor. China became a republic in 1912, but it was still dominated by Japan and powerful nations in Europe. In the late 1920s, Mao led a guerilla war against the Chinese Nationalist government. After defeating the United States–supported Nationalist forces in 1949, Mao declared the birth of the People's Republic. Che, and many others, admired Mao. They did not see the ill effects Mao's actions had on many of his people. Mao's attempt to bring farming and industry under the control of the government resulted in a famine that caused the deaths of 20 million people. As in any dictatorship, any opposition to Mao's rule was severely punished.

Mao achieved great things for China, but progress came at a great cost for many Chinese people.

CAUGHT!

In May 1956, Mexican police suddenly rounded up Fidel, Raúl, Che, and most of the other revolutionaries. The Mexican government captured the rebels to please Batista and the Cuban government. Batista realized that Fidel's group was planning another revolution.

Che spent about two months in a Mexican jail. He and Fidel shared a cell at one point, and the experience brought them

A Born Rebel

Fidel Castro was a guerilla fighter who became Cuba's 22nd president. The dictator, who ruled from 1959 to 2008, was a rebel from his earliest days. He once organized farm workers against his father and led them in a strike for

better wages! He remained very much a rebel his entire life, standing out in a time when communism had fallen from favor worldwide. Fidel seemed to enjoy his status and liked to maintain his revolutionary image. Even as head of Cuba, he continued to wear fatigues every day.

Fidel Castro (on left, third from bottom) and his revolutionaries were rather conscious about their image. The Cuban rebels were fond of olive-green fatigues and huge cigars, both of which became their trademarks.

closer together. At the time, Fidel was 29 years old and Che was 26. Physically they were different. Temperamentally, they were a good match. Both were uncompromising men who believed in sacrificing for a greater good. Both were tough on themselves, pushing themselves to the limit, physically and otherwise.

Fidel was released from jail first. Che feared he would be left behind when the rebels left for Cuba. Fidel assured him, however, that the revolution would not start without him. Che finally got out of jail by telling the authorities he was just a tourist. He was ready for the greatest adventure of his life. He was about to help liberate Cuba from the dictatorship of Batista.

Everyone's Buddy

It was around the time that Ernesto was released from jail that he started to be known as "Che." That means "buddy" in Argentine slang. The Cuban revolutionaries heard Ernesto use this expression so many times that they gave it to him as his nickname. It was a name the whole world would soon come to know.

THE REVOLUTIONARIES SET SAIL

Early in the morning of November 25, 1956, the men of the 26th of July Movement boarded a yacht called the *Granma*. The boat was built to carry only about 10 people. That morning it held 82 men plus all their weapons, food, ammunition, and other equipment.

As the boat motored out of the Mexican city of Tuxpan, Che realized he had left his asthma inhaler behind. The voyage across the Gulf of Mexico was one of the most harrowing experiences of his life. For six days, Che lay on the deck, sometimes vomiting, sometimes just gasping for breath.

Che had signed on as a revolutionary. Because he had a medical degree, he had been given the title of medical officer for the expedition. Now the doctor was too sick to offer help to anyone else—and the others did need it. The seas were rough, and many of the men got sick.

Days passed as the *Granma* made slow progress across the Caribbean Sea. Each plane that passed overhead caused great anxiety. The men feared that the Cuban military was looking for them. If a plane happened to spot the *Granma*, the ship would surely be blown out of the water. Wind and waves caused anxiety, too. The *Granma* was not built to hold so many passengers. It tossed and heaved violently with the waves. So did the men. At times, Castro ordered the men to throw things overboard to lighten the load and keep the boat upright.

Finally, late on the night of December 1, lookouts saw lights dead ahead. They had reached Cuba's southwest coast. They

Cubans still celebrate around the Granma, *the leaky yacht that carried Castro, Che, and 80 other revolutionaries across the Gulf of Mexico to Cuba in 1956.*

just weren't sure where. Between the choppy seas and trying to avoid military planes, the men had gotten off course. Suddenly there was a splash. The navigator had been leaning over the side of the boat searching for a landmark when he fell overboard. The *Granma* completed three circles before the navigator was located and fished out of the sea. By that time, it was too late to look for the proper landing spot. Day would be breaking soon. With it would come the scout planes of the Cuban air force. The revolutionaries had to get ashore.

The *Granma* came to ground in the early morning hours of December 2. The boat landed in the wet sand of an area the locals called Las Coloradas. Che and the others leapt off the boat and into a murky swamp. The going would be tough, but it was too late to turn around. They had to keep pressing forward.

Daylight found the revolutionaries 2 miles (3.2 km) inland. The men were weary and footsore from the slow march through the muck. Suddenly they heard military airplanes overhead.

The Last Voyage of the Granma

The voyage of the 26th of July Movement was the last for the *Granma*. In 1959, after the success of the revolution, the *Granma* was brought to Havana, Cuba's capital city. It remains there today as a memorial to the revolutionaries of 1956. A replica of the *Granma* is located near the beach where it landed.

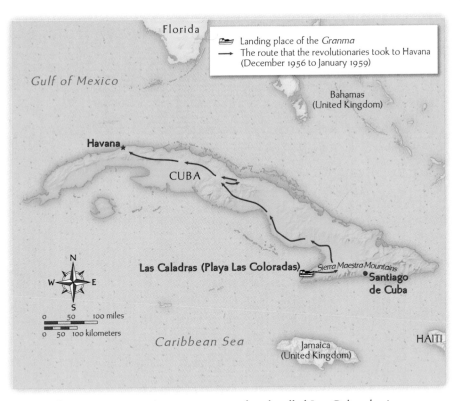

The revolutionaries came ashore at a swampy beach called Las Coloradas in
December 1956. Two years and one month later, they entered Havana in triumph.

Cuba's military leaders suspected the revolutionaries might try
to land in this region. Early that morning, scout planes located
the deserted *Granma*. It didn't take long for them to track the soldiers and bring more planes into the search. As the planes drew
nearer, the revolutionaries took cover. They realized the *Granma*
had been spotted and they were being tracked. The men were
keenly aware that there was no escape. Their only options were
victory or death. For the moment, though, their strategy was to
run. They made their way inland as fast as they could. ❖

Fidel Castro (front) was a tireless leader. His absolute self-confidence was equaled by Che's daredevil spirit. The two men got along well.

CHAPTER SIX

THE CUBAN REVOLUTION

FOR THREE DAYS, THE REVOLUTIONARIES KEPT constantly on the move. They tried to keep off the beaten path, usually marching through rarely traveled forests and meadows. They did everything they could to stay one step ahead of the Cuban planes. They knew that Cuban military and police forces were close by. They did not know just how close. They found out late in the afternoon on December 5, 1956. The Cuban military caught the revolutionaries completely by surprise. Fidel later recalled:

We all dispersed, like crazy. I stayed more or less where I was, with two compañeros, in the cane field where some of our men had taken shelter—some of them had run right through it. Each man or small group had its own battle to fight.

The battle, which happened out of the blue, took place in an area called Allegre de Pio. Years later, Che recalled the moment when his band was overtaken by the enemy:

> *Comrade Montane and I were leaning against a tree,*
> *talking about our respective children; we were eating our*
> *meager rations—half a sausage and two crackers—when*
> *we heard a shot. In a matter of seconds a hurricane of*
> *bullets—or at least this is what it seemed to my anxious*
> *mind during that trial by fire—rained on the troop of*
> *eighty-two men.*

In the seconds that followed the first round of fire, Che realized he had both a box of ammunition and a medical bag at his feet.

Che's adventurous spirit was always offset by his studious side. When in camp, Che (left) could often be found reading while the others socialized.

There was no time to rescue both. He had to make a choice. Che seized the cartridge box and hastened to the woods. He later recalled making that fateful choice between being a doctor and a soldier:

This was perhaps the first time I was faced with the dilemma of choosing between my dedication to medicine and my duty as a revolutionary soldier. At my feet were a pack full of medicines and a cartridge box. I chose the cartridge box, leaving behind the medicine pack.

As Che hurried toward the woods, he felt the sting of bullets. "I felt a terrible blow on the chest and another in the neck," he later wrote, "and was sure I was dead."

Che's wounds were minor. He had just been grazed by the bullets. To Che's anxious mind—caught in his first real battle—it seemed like the end, however. He prepared to meet his death like a man. The last words he heard during the ambush were those of a comrade who called out, "Here no one surrenders."

> **"Here no one surrenders."**
>
> – REVOLUTIONARY

Che would not surrender, and he would not die with his back to a Cuban tree. He would defy fate this day, as would Fidel and a handful of others. Three small groups of revolutionaries, led by Fidel, Raúl, and Che, escaped the ambush. There was little reason to believe they would survive for long. Batista's military had done its work well. About 60 of the 82 men had been killed or captured. The men who were captured suffered terrible torture at the hands of Batista's police.

Viva la Revolution!

Americans watching from a distance had mixed feelings about the Cuban Revolution. Fulgencio Batista's government was friendly to American business interests, and many Americans enjoyed vacationing in Cuba. When news came that a tiny group of 82 men were trying to overthrow such a powerful government and military, however, quite a few Americans came to admire the revolutionaries, at least from a safe distance. The legend of Che Guevara would only grow from there.

TRIAL BY FIRE

The next two weeks were a time of trial for all three groups. The men, who had to keep on the move, had no food. They lived on roots, grass, and sometimes tree bark. Finally, the groups came together around dawn on December 21. Until the reunion with Fidel, Che had been the commander of his small group. If he expected praise for keeping his men alive, he was disappointed. Fidel reprimanded him for having lost his gun in the skirmish. For a while, Che was in a state of disgrace.

By January 1957, Che, Fidel, and about a dozen other revolutionaries were in the Sierra Maestra mountains of southwest Cuba. This rugged, beautiful mountain range extends for more than 100 miles (161 km), running parallel to the sea.

The people of the Sierra Maestra were among the poorest of Cuba's poor. Many had never seen a doctor in their lives. Che—who continually played two roles, one as fighter and one as doctor—ministered to many of them. Some of the mountain people became very loyal to Castro and the idea of his revolution. Others betrayed the revolutionaries. Many times, in the winter and spring of 1957, the guerrillas were on the run.

Che's role was constantly changing. First he had been the medical doctor, then a leader of a small band. Then there was the period when Che was out of favor with Fidel. By the late spring of 1957, Che had become the leader's second-most trusted man

Peasants in the Sierra Maestra lived desperately difficult lives. Che did everything he could for them—as a doctor and as a soldier.

after his brother Raúl. By the summer, Che was given the title of commandante. Years later, Fidel recalled the special qualities that made Che so important to the movement:

> *Che carried out the mission I'd sent him on. The battle
> at Uvero lasted about three hours. The enemy had eleven
> dead and nineteen wounded, among them the lieutenant
> commanding the barracks. We lost seven combatants
> and had eight wounded, several of them seriously. Once
> we'd achieved our victory, we provided aid to those who
> needed it. Che and the garrison doctor treated the enemy*

Che and Fidel became even closer friends during the year they spent together in the mountains.

wounded, which there were more of than our own, and then they treated ours. Che treated all of them. You can't imagine that man's sensitivity.

Fidel spoke of Che's good qualities. But a darker side to his personality was also emerging. In the spring of 1957, the revolutionaries were often betrayed by local peasants. Some men also deserted the movement. On one occasion, Che shot a deserter as an example to the others. Nothing in his diary or letters suggests that he felt badly about it.

FIGHTING TYRANNY

The revolutionaries didn't think it would be easy to overthrow Batista's regime. Few of them knew quite how difficult it would be. Throughout 1957, the revolutionaries were in the Sierra Maestra. Moving to lower ground would invite attacks. Many days went by with little to eat. There were times when everyone—except Fidel—was genuinely desperate.

Che continued to double as the medical officer and a guerrilla fighter. Several times, he participated in long, slogging battles, only to follow up by tending the wounded of both sides. Later, he described a typical scene following a battle:

While the B-26s were buzzing the sawmill in search of victims, we were calmly having our breakfast; installed in various parts of the building, we drank hot chocolate brought to us by the mistress of the house—who was not exactly cheered by the sight of the B-26s passing and re-passing, almost grazing the roof.

Che loved horses, and he also needed them. There were times when his asthma was so painful that riding was the only way he could get around.

Che continued to suffer from asthma. He didn't complain, though, at least not much. He struggled to keep up with his fellow revolutionaries. There were times, sometimes as long as a week, when he simply could not walk. There were times when he was left behind and had to catch up with the rest of the men later. On some occasions, Che's comrades carried him. Whenever possible, he rode a horse.

The situation looked grim for the revolutionaries, but then things turned around in the autumn of 1958. Batista sent 10,000 well-armed, well-supplied army troops to trap the revolutionaries in their mountain strongholds. Fidel and Che's "army" amounted to only about 200 fighters. With the help of the local people, however, they were able to outmaneuver and surprise the enemy, time and again. By December, Batista's men were in full retreat, and the revolutionaries had come down from the mountains in pursuit.

Fidel and one group of revolutionaries went east to attack Santiago de Cuba. Che led another group to attack Havana, Cuba's capital. The way there was not easy, but Che won a big victory at Santa Clara at the end of December. On January 3, 1959, he entered the fortress that guards Havana. The Argentine doctor had become a Cuban revolutionary hero. ❖

In 1959, Che entered Havana to become that city's military ruler. The 30-year-old revolutionary had come very far very fast.

CHAPTER SEVEN

CHE IN CHARGE

C UBA'S DICTATOR FULGENCIO BATISTA FLED
the country for the Dominican Republic on New Year's
Day 1959. The 26th of July Movement was now in
control of Cuba. Che, the new revolutionary hero, was in charge
of the fortress that guards Havana. This was the most power he
ever had. Che's behavior over the next three months was considered by some to be an abuse of this new-found might. During
that time, Che presided over a series of trials and hearings that
sent about 500 people to the firing squads. Sometimes the hearings
were lengthy, with evidence presented on both sides. Sometimes
they were swift, with vengeance seeming as important as justice.
Some people found Che's ruthlessness shocking. He was not the
only revolutionary commander to exercise this type of power.
Because the hearings were in Havana, however, Che's actions
attracted the greatest attention.

Years later, a close friend asked Che if he had gone too far in ordering so many executions. "Look," Che replied, "in this thing you have to kill before they kill you." He knew from experience that a leader who let his enemies live might someday come to regret it. The 26th of July Movement was the perfect example of this. Batista released the Castro brothers from jail soon after their first attempted coup in 1953. The brothers regrouped in Mexico and reformed their revolutionary band—this time with Che as a member. Three years later, the Castros returned to Cuba at the head of the 26th of July Movement and launched a successful revolution.

> **"You have to kill before they kill you."**
>
> – CHE GUEVARA

FAMILY MATTERS

The Guevara family flew in from Argentina to visit Che soon after he took control of Havana. Che's tough new attitude must have come as a surprise to his parents, who hadn't seen their son since he left home six years earlier. Che had an emotional reunion with his mother and sister, but his relationship with his father was strained. Ernesto Sr. had a bad habit of claiming his son's success as his own. The two clashed on several occasions. Che's mother would return to Cuba to visit her son in the future. This was the last time Che would ever see his father, however.

During this time, Che was also reunited with his wife Hilda and his daughter Hildita. The reunion was brief. Immediately upon Hilda's arrival, Che told her he had fallen in love with another woman. Her name was Aleida March. Aleida was Cuban. She

In the winter of 1959, Ernesto Sr. and Celia flew to Cuba to visit their son. This visit was the last time Che would ever see his father.

had joined the revolution in 1958 and had won respect for her willingness to take risks. Several times, she had hid ammunition and supplies under her skirt to carry them to the revolutionaries. Aleida and Che met by chance. Soon after, she became his secretary. Romance blossomed, and the two began a relationship even though Che was already married. Hilda was heartbroken, but she knew she had no chance of winning back Che's affections. She agreed to separate. The couple divorced in May 1959. Just one month later, Che and Aleida were married.

Aleida had won Che's heart, but she, like Hilda before her, would soon learn that work always came first with her new husband. Just two weeks after their wedding, Che flew off on a series of diplomatic missions.

AN UNLIKELY DIPLOMAT

Che had always been an enthusiastic traveler. Now he had an opportunity to combine two of his great loves. He could see the world while helping build the new state of Cuba. In his first year as Cuba's ambassador, Che went to Paris, Moscow, and even Peking, China. He met the leaders of Soviet Russia, as well as his hero Mao Zedong, the head of Communist China. Wherever he went Che was asked by the press whether he was a communist. His answer was always yes. When he was asked about the new Cuban government, Che was more careful. Fidel had not yet decided to align himself with the Communist Bloc nations.

The Cold War

The Cold War began in 1946 and lasted until 1991. This period was called a cold war because it didn't involve any military action. The Cold War pitted communist countries, such as the Soviet Union, against democratic nations such as the United States. For 45 years, the Communist Bloc nations of Russia, Yugoslavia, China, and others were opposed to the capitalistic democracies of Britain, Germany, the United States, and others. Che was vocal about which side he favored—the communists. Fidel Castro took longer, until about 1961, to make up his mind. After Mikhail Gorbachev came to power in Russia in 1985, he worked with President Ronald Reagan to end the Cold War.

By 1960, Che's beret with the star on it was becoming his trademark. So was his smile, which Time *magazine called "devastating."*

Fidel had come to power in Cuba at the height of the Cold War (1946–1991). At the time, communism was considered the biggest threat to American security. Much of the focus of United States leaders during this period was to make sure that communism did not spread to other countries around the globe. Dwight D. Eisenhower was the U.S. president when Castro took over Cuba. He had good reason to worry about whether a country so close to the United States would become communist. It is surprising that Che showed so much tact when asked about Fidel's political position. He wasn't usually so diplomatic. He took his new role as a representative of Cuba very seriously. He was also very loyal

Cuba's Early History

The official name of Cuba is *República de Cuba*, or Republic of Cuba. The country was under Spanish rule for about 400 years and became very profitable for its production of sugar. Great numbers of slaves—whether of Native American or African descent—labored in the sugar plantations until Spain finally outlawed slavery in the 19th century. By then, it was too late to reverse the economic and social trend, which led to a rich upper class, an extremely poor working class, and very few people in between. Cuba fought two wars of independence in the late nineteenth century. The island finally won independence from Spain in 1902. Close relations between the United States and Cuba developed during the 1930s and 1940s. The American government even supported Batista, who was seen as the most pro-United States and pro-business of all Cuban leaders.

to his friend Fidel. He was careful not to cause the new leader any trouble. Fidel returned Che's loyalty and rewarded him with even more power in the new government.

In an unlikely move, Fidel made Che the finance minister of Cuba. Ironically, the man who hated money, class, and social distinctions was in charge of the country's wealth. As minister of the National Bank, Che had his face plastered on the new Cuban paper money notes. As was the custom, the notes also featured Che's signature. Instead of using the formal, dignified signature "Ernesto Guevara de la Serna," he simply signed the notes "Che." It was his way of saying that, though he was minister of finance, he still despised the class distinctions money brought about. Che would always align himself with the common man. To him, Cuba was only in the beginning stage of what he thought would be a permanent revolution, one to sweep away class and economic distinctions.

Just a few months later, Che was made minister of industries. He was an unusual type of cabinet minister. He worked long hours at his desk. He also spent at least one day a week laboring with peasants in the sugar cane fields. Che believed he had to lead by example. He also believed in equality. Even though he was a government official, Che never felt that he was better than anyone else, including the Cuban working class.

In August 1960, Che was featured on the cover of *Time* magazine. The essay described the three men in charge of Cuba:

Prime Minister Castro, at 33, is the heart, soul, voice, and bearded visage of present-day Cuba. His younger brother, Armed Forces Chief Raúl Castro, 29, is the fist that holds the revolution's dagger. National Bank President Che Guevara, 32, is the brain. It is he who is most responsible for driving Cuba sharply left, away from the U.S. that he despises and into a volunteered alliance with Russia. He is the most fascinating, and the most dangerous, member of the triumvirate.

Che loved his children, but spent only a small portion of his time with them. Revolution, and the business of governing Cuba, came first.

The magazine also noted Che's strong personal qualities. He was at his desk longer than almost anyone else in the government, and friends called him incorruptible. Che never used his power or position to help relatives or friends. None of this came as a surprise to the people who knew Che best. Nothing was more important to him than achieving the goals of the revolution.

Che's attitude made family life difficult. The work of the revolution always came first. He did love his children. In addition to the one daughter he had with Hilda, Che had four children with Aleida. The couple had two girls named Aleida and Celia and two boys, Camilo and Ernesto. Che worked long hours, so Aleida had to do almost all the work of raising the children. Che even missed the birth of two of his children because he was out of the country on diplomatic missions. When he was at home, though, Che was a good father. He loved playing with his kids and reading to them. Yet these moments were rare compared to the far more time-consuming business of helping to run a new communist country. As a new decade dawned and friction between the United States and Cuba increased, Che's work concerns would become even more pressing.

TROUBLE WITH THE UNITED STATES

In 1960, Castro began making moves that caused the United States government to grow worried. Cuba was importing oil from the Soviet Union. When American refineries in Cuba refused to process the Soviet oil, the Cuban government took over the companies. Castro followed this by nationalizing other American companies in Cuba without offering any financial compensation. Even worse in the eyes of the United States government was the relationship developing between Cuba and the Soviet Union.

In October, President Eisenhower placed a trade embargo on the island nation. The United States would no longer import goods from Cuba. In January 1961, Castro made a speech in which he claimed the United States embassy in Cuba was filled with spies. He demanded that the staff there be cut from 87 people to 11. The following morning President Eisenhower broke off diplomatic relations with Cuba.

At the time, Eisenhower was on his way out of office. The new president, John F. Kennedy, had his own plans for bringing Cuba

Castro's Cuba

Fidel (right) ruled Cuba from 1959 until he transferred power to Raúl (left) in 2008. Cuba still does not have diplomatic relations with the United States. A United States trade blockade has caused hardship to the island and its people. Still, the overall standard of living has improved throughout the years of communist rule. With that improvement comes a loss of many freedoms, however.

In a communist country, the government controls schools and health services. All citizens receive an education and have access to health care. On the other hand, they are not allowed to speak out against the government. There is no freedom of the press, and there are no free elections.

Cuban citizens are not allowed to leave the country without permission, but that does not stop the thousands who flee the island each year. Many risk everything they have— including their lives—for a chance to live in freedom.

back into line. Together with the Central Intelligence Agency (CIA), Kennedy was planning to overthrow the government.

The CIA had been training about 2,000 Cuban exiles in Florida and Guatemala. These men, who had been expelled from Cuba, were being taught how to fight. Right after he was inaugurated, President Kennedy put together a plan for the exiles to invade Cuba.

THE BAY OF PIGS

On the morning of April 17, 1961, Che awoke to the sound of airplanes overhead and gunfire in the distance. The American-backed Cuban exiles had landed on Cuba's southern coast, at a place called Playa Giron, on the Bay of Pigs.

Che rushed to the battlefront, as did Fidel and most of the other leaders of the Cuban Revolution. The fighting was heavy, but there was little doubt as to the outcome. The United States had failed to provide air support to the Cuban exiles. If they had, the Bay of Pigs might have resulted in victory for America. Instead it became the country's most bitter defeat. At the end of two days of fighting, the exiles were nearly all killed, captured, or wounded. ❖

Che didn't trust Russian dictator Nikita Khrushchev (right). His instincts were proven right when the Soviets let Cuba down during the Cuban Missile Crisis in 1962.

CHAPTER EIGHT

TO THE BRINK

IN THE SUMMER OF 1962, CHE TOOK HIS THIRD
trip to the Soviet Union. Che never liked or trusted Russian
Premier Nikita Khrushchev, but he was there on a special
mission for Fidel. Cuba was having great economic difficulties.
America had always been a large importer of Cuban sugar. Now
the economic blockade the United States had imposed on Cuban
products was wrecking the Cuban economy. Che went to Russia
to put together a trade agreement. He was hoping the Soviets
would buy the sugar that the Americans were refusing to import.
The Russians were happy to trade with the Cubans. Khrushchev
was even happier to have a communist ally so close to his country's American enemy.

When Fidel sent Che to Russia, he wasn't just looking for
a trade partner. He was also looking for a bargaining tool, a
means by which to threaten America. He wanted the Russians to

place missiles in Cuba. Che did not have a hard time convincing the Russians of this plan. The Americans already had missiles, and nuclear weapons, in Turkey. Those missiles were very close to the Soviet Union. The Russians were eager to have powerful weapons of their own close to American soil. By the time Che returned from his trip, the first Russian ships carrying missiles were already steaming toward Cuba.

THE CUBAN MISSILE CRISIS

What Che, Fidel, and the Russians did not know was that American spy planes had been keeping a close eye on Cuba. Dozens, if not hundreds, of American planes flew over Cuba every week. Many of them brought back high-quality photographs of what was happening below. By early October, President Kennedy and his Cabinet knew that Russian missiles

Alternate Realities

In 1957, President Eisenhower offered missiles to America's allies in Europe. Turkey was one country that accepted the offer. Some people believe that placing Russian missiles in Cuba was no different than placing U.S. missiles in Turkey. American officials argued, however, that the missiles in Turkey were defensive—they were meant to prevent an attack from Russia. They said that Russian missiles in Cuba were offensive—placed there to start a war.

LAUNCH POSITION

MISSILE-READY TENTS

MISSILE ERECTORS

*Spy photos like this one persuaded the United Nations, and the world at large,
that Russia and Cuba intended to use nuclear weapons against the United States.*

had been placed on the island. They also knew that other Russian ships, carrying nuclear warheads, were on the way.

President Kennedy went into emergency mode. He summoned his advisers and began to work out a strategy to peacefully resolve the issue. At a visit to the United Nations, the American ambassador boldly claimed that there were Russian missiles in Cuba. Then he displayed the aerial photographs that backed up his accusation. Interestingly, the ambassador's argument was directed against the Russians. He did not accuse the Cuban government of any wrongdoing. President Kennedy went on television to announce a blockade of Cuba. No ships—Russian or otherwise—would be allowed near the island.

Meanwhile, on the island, Che and Fidel were preparing for the worst. They went into full crisis mode, as if they were on the brink of war. They built bunkers in caves where they could make their headquarters during the fighting. These hideaways were equipped with cots and telephones so the leaders could stay in touch. They also made sure their army was ready to fend off an attack. It was as if they expected the entire United States Army to descend on Cuba at any moment. In fact, Che, Fidel, and the other Cuban leaders were hoping there would be a fight. They saw this as their great moment, one in which they and their Soviet allies could make the Americans back down. It was not to be, however.

During the Cuban Missile Crisis, Che's headquarters was a bunker (right) hidden inside the Los Portales caves.

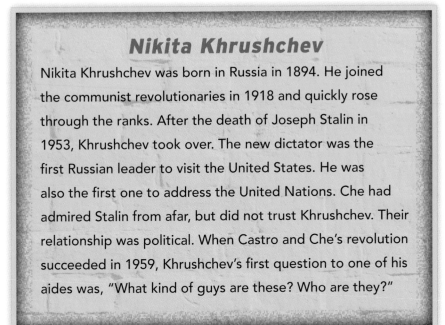

Nikita Khrushchev

Nikita Khrushchev was born in Russia in 1894. He joined the communist revolutionaries in 1918 and quickly rose through the ranks. After the death of Joseph Stalin in 1953, Khrushchev took over. The new dictator was the first Russian leader to visit the United States. He was also the first one to address the United Nations. Che had admired Stalin from afar, but did not trust Khrushchev. Their relationship was political. When Castro and Che's revolution succeeded in 1959, Khrushchev's first question to one of his aides was, "What kind of guys are these? Who are they?"

QUARANTINE

President Kennedy did not call for an invasion of Cuba. Had he done so, the United States would have looked like a bully for attacking such a small neighbor. Instead, he directed all his conversations toward the Soviet Union, making the case that it was Premier Khrushchev who had brought about the crisis.

United States ships quickly took up patrol stations all around Cuba. Kennedy did not call the maneuver a blockade—which would have had military implications. Instead, he claimed the action was a quarantine of Cuba. This was an odd choice of words. *Quarantine* is a medical term, meaning to separate someone infected with a disease to keep it from spreading. The strategy worked.

A Russian ship heads for Cuba while an American plane flies overhead. The Missile Crisis was a frightening time for Americans, Russians, and Cubans.

A DEADLY GAME OF CHICKEN

As American ships patrolled the seas around Cuba and American planes filled the skies, Cuban men and women prepared for an imminent assault. Che, at least, was ready—even anxious—for an attack. He had never really had the opportunity to fight Americans in the field. He itched for the opportunity.

Fidel also expected—and looked forward to—a big fight. He had taken a great gamble in inviting the Russians to Cuba. He believed the U.S. attack would come, but it was Khrushchev who had the final say.

From the relative safety of Moscow, Khrushchev saw his plan unraveling. He had hoped that the United States would invade Cuba. That would have made the Americans look like aggressive imperialists in the eyes of the world. President Kennedy had outmaneuvered him. The United States was showing restraint in dealing with its tiny island neighbor. People around the world rallied around the United States in what was increasingly seen as a Russian-created crisis. Khrushchev also realized that he had little to gain from a war with the United States.

On October 27, just miles before they would have encountered the American quarantine, the Russians ships turned around and sailed away. Weeks later, the Russian missiles were removed from Cuba. The crisis was resolved in 13 days. To the parties involved, it only seemed a lot longer.

Behind the Scenes

For many years, people wondered whether President Kennedy and Soviet Premier Khrushchev made a behind-the-scenes deal to end the Cuban Missile Crisis. The answer was revealed when the tape recordings of President Kennedy's National Security Council were declassified. The tapes revealed that Kennedy agreed to remove American missiles from Turkey as long as the Russians took theirs out of Cuba. Part of the agreement was that the deal would remain a secret.

Never before had the world been closer to an all-out nuclear war. The crisis had come and gone without a hostile shot being fired. Americans, Russians, and most Cubans all breathed much easier.

Che and Fidel, on the other hand, were furious. The Russians had let them down. Fidel later recalled:

We learned from news reports that the Soviets were making the proposal to withdraw the missiles. And it had never been discussed with us in any way! We weren't opposed to a solution, because it was important to avoid a nuclear conflict. But Khrushchev should have told the Americans, 'The Cubans must be involved in the discussions.' At that moment they lost their nerve, and they weren't firm in their determination. Out of principle, they should have consulted with us.

Che, as usual, was more radical in his reaction. He told a newspaper reporter, "If the missiles had remained we would have used them against the very heart of the U.S., including New York City."

LOOKING FOR A FIGHT

The two years that followed the Cuban Missile Crisis were frustrating for Che. He was a man of action and was bored with his government work.

Fidel and Che remained as close as ever, but their paths were about to diverge. Fidel had always been, primarily, a Cuban patriot. His greatest goal had been the overthrow of Batista and the creation of a new government. By 1960, Fidel had succeeded in many, if not most, of his goals. Che, on the other hand, was not tied to any particular nation. He wanted to start a worldwide revolution.

In 1964, the United States entered a long, undeclared war against North Vietnam, in Southeast Asia. Right from the beginning, Che saw the Vietnam War as a way to deplete American resources. He hoped to further weaken the country by getting the United States involved in numerous wars around the globe. In an essay, he called for revolutionaries around the world to create "one, two, three, many Vietnams." At the same time, Che called for a "Tricontinental" strategy. This meant that revolutionaries should create insurgent movements on three continents at once: Asia, Africa, and South America.

> "If the missiles had remained [in Cuba] we would have used them against the heart of the U.S., including New York City."
>
> – CHE GUEVARA

It was one thing to call for worldwide revolution. It was another to lead one. Che could not be in all places at once. He had to make a choice. In the spring of 1965, Che set his sights on the Congo in central Africa.

After making his decision, Che composed two letters. He sent one to Fidel, letting his friend know that he was leaving Cuba. To make a complete break, Che resigned all his offices and positions in Cuba. He even renounced his Cuban citizenship. This would keep Fidel, and Cuba, from becoming entangled in Che's future revolutionary work.

Che also sent a letter to his children. They were instructed to not open the letter unless Che failed to return from his mission. He wrote:

> *Dear Hildita, Aliedita, Camilo, Celia and Ernesto,*
>
> *If you read this letter one day, it will mean that I am no longer alive. You will hardly remember me, and the smallest among you will have entirely forgotten me.*
>
> *Your father was a man who acted as he thought best and who has been absolutely faithful to his convictions.*
>
> *Grow up into good revolutionaries. Study hard to master technique, which gives you mastery over nature. Remember that it is the Revolution which is important and that each of us, taken in isolation, is worth nothing. Above all be sensitive, in the deepest areas of yourselves, to any injustices committed against whoever it may be anywhere in the world.*
>
> *Yours always, my children. I hope to see you again.*
> *A big strong kiss from Daddy.*

THE CONGO

Che arrived at Lake Tanganyika, on the eastern side of the Congo, in the spring of 1965. He had about 20 Cuban guerrilla fighters with him, men whom he trusted to the utmost. They felt the same way about him.

The situation in the Congo was not very straightforward. There were no less than three revolutionary groups, all hoping to overthrow the dictatorship of Joseph Mobutu. The Cubans

Even when leading a guerrilla force in the Congo, Che took time out to visit with the locals and befriend children. Oddly, Che's humane role as a doctor went hand-in-hand with his violent role as a revolutionary.

came ready to fight, but they found that the local people were not eager to join. The dictatorial government was absolutely ruthless in its treatment of captured rebels. Few people came forward to join the revolutionary cause.

Weeks, then months, passed. Che kept receiving more fighters from Cuba, but he was also losing men to death, desertion, and disease. Once again, Che was both the medical doctor and the leader of his revolutionary band. His soldiers could not go on like this for long. After a little more than a year, Che realized he had to give up his dream of a revolution in the Congo.

In the winter of 1966, Che recrossed Lake Tanganyika and flew to Eastern Europe. In the entire year he had been in Africa, Che's enemies in the CIA had been unable to track him, but

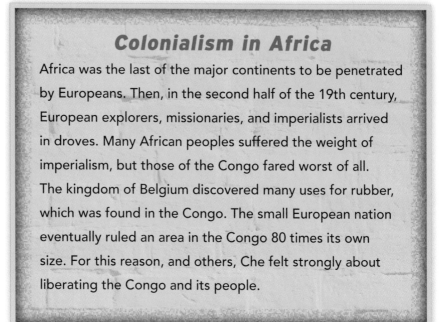

Colonialism in Africa

Africa was the last of the major continents to be penetrated by Europeans. Then, in the second half of the 19th century, European explorers, missionaries, and imperialists arrived in droves. Many African peoples suffered the weight of imperialism, but those of the Congo fared worst of all. The kingdom of Belgium discovered many uses for rubber, which was found in the Congo. The small European nation eventually ruled an area in the Congo 80 times its own size. For this reason, and others, Che felt strongly about liberating the Congo and its people.

now they were close behind. Ever since the Bay of Pigs invasion, a handful of Cuban exiles had devoted themselves to tracking down Che for the United States government.

CHE'S NEXT MISSION

Che flew back to Cuba, where he met in secret with Fidel. He had no plans to stay there, though. Because of his role as a revolutionary leader from 1956 to 1959, Che could have had a very comfortable life in Cuba, but that did not interest him. He believed there were still battles to be fought for poor and oppressed people around the world.

As Che planned his next move, he decided to go to Bolivia. He knew he would never reach the South American country undetected without an elaborate disguise, though. To change from a long-haired revolutionary into a balding Bolivian businessman, Che plucked most of his hair out, strand by strand. Che Guevara, the most dangerous man in the world, was transformed into Ramon. The disguise was so thorough, so complete, that most of Che's guerrilla warriors did not recognize him when they first saw him. In the autumn of 1966, "Ramon" flew from Cuba to La Paz, the capital of Bolivia. ❖

After the revolution, Che became a wanted man. He had to use clever disguises to keep would-be assassins off his tail.

CHAPTER NINE

The Making of an Icon

AFTER LANDING IN THE BOLIVIAN CAPITAL, CHE headed for the countryside. His plan was to spark a new revolution against global capitalism and the United States. This time, unlike in the Congo, Che seemed to have some advantages. He had been invited to the country by the Communist Party of Bolivia. Party members told him that many Bolivian peasants were eager to bring about a revolution. Che also had most of his best men, guerrilla fighters who had been with him during the toughest days of the Cuban Revolution. He was in contact with Fidel by radio, and Fidel was ready to send him more men when the moment was right. Unfortunately, all Che's plans quickly unravelled.

The Communist Party leader and Che disliked each other from the start. The Communist Party ended up abandoning Che and his men in the Bolivian countryside. Che didn't mind working

Che only seemed to be full of confidence and enthusiasm in Bolivia. His experiences there were wearing him down—physically and psychologically.

alone. He and his followers had even established a good base of operations in the Bolivian mountains. Then they were spotted by Bolivian army planes. Before long, Che and his men were on the run—and Che's asthma was worse than ever. There were times in the winter of 1966–1967 when he could neither stand up nor ride. There were times when he could barely speak. Che also lost radio contact with Fidel. He was now completely on his own.

AN OLD ENEMY RETURNS

The CIA had long wished to kill or capture Che. In the spring of 1967, they learned he was in Bolivia. Not only did the Bolivian military wish to assist the CIA, but a handful of Cuban exiles—men who remembered Che from the Bay of Pigs—were eager to get at him, too.

In the late summer of 1967, the CIA and Bolivian military found Che's trail. They learned from deserters that the rebel leader was suffering from severe asthma attacks and that the morale of his men was low. This was the time to close in for the kill. The Bolivian military men and a handful of CIA operatives ran Che and his band to the ground on October 7, 1967. There was a short fight, in which several revolutionaries were killed. Che and several other men fell into the hands of the enemy.

CHE'S LAST HOURS

The two eyewitness accounts of Che's last hours differ in some respects. One was written by a Bolivian army colonel, the other by the CIA agent Felix Rodriguez. The accounts agree that Che was defiant to the end. When asked how he ended up a prisoner, he replied flatly that he had failed. When asked why he had come all the way from Cuba, he answered that it was to free the Bolivian peasants. The accounts also agree that Che was in terrible shape. His clothing was largely shredded, and even his boots were gone, replaced by strips of rubber. Months of being on the run, combating asthma all the while, had taken a powerful toll.

The Bolivian army colonel and his men had orders to kill Che. They left the actual killing to the CIA operative and his men. Sometime on the afternoon of October 9, 1967, Felix Rodriguez had his last conversation with Che. The revolutionary knew the end was near. He and Rodriguez became almost pleasant to one another, and then the Cuban-born CIA man left the building. He was replaced by a Bolivian sergeant who was eager to put an end to the great Che Guevara. No one can be sure just what Che's last words were, but, according to legend, he said, "I know why you've come. Shoot, coward, you are only going to kill a man."

A HERO'S DEATH

The news of Che's death spread rapidly. *The New York Times* ran photos of Che, in his last hours, on October 11. Public response was sympathetic to Che and against the Bolivian military. It helped Che's cause that America's war in Vietnam was entering its most unpopular phase. A huge student demonstration against the war took place in Washington, D.C., on Sunday, October 22. As thousands of people stood near the Lincoln Memorial, John Wilson, director of the Students Nonviolent Coordinating Committee addressed the crowd. He asked for a moment of silence to mark Che's death.

> **"I know why you've come. Shoot, coward, you are only going to kill a man."**
>
> – CHE GUEVARA

Mainstream newspapers and magazines were less sympathetic to the man and his cause. *Time* magazine gave this verdict:

> *Che's death will hardly mean the end of Communist activity in Latin America. There are still deep-rooted conditions of poverty, neglect, and hopelessness that subversives can feed on and exploit. But his departure from the scene takes away much of the mystery and romanticism that has been associated with that subversion.*

At first, Fidel refused to believe Che was gone. The Argentine had seemed indestructible. When he learned the truth, Fidel gave his departed comrade a splendid funeral in Havana (even though Che was buried in Bolivia). In his eulogy, Fidel portrayed Che as the symbol of the "New Man" Cuba hoped to foster. He said in part:

> *If we wish to express what we expect our revolutionary combatants, our militants, our men to be, we must say, without hesitation: 'Let them be like Che!' If we wish to express what we want the men of future generations to be, we must say: 'Let them be like Che!'*

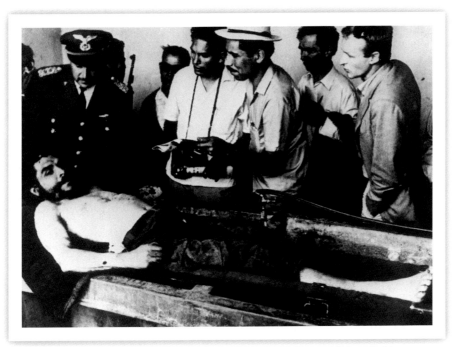

A photo of Che's lifeless body was shown all around the world. It won him a great deal of sympathy and made the Bolivian military look like heartless killers.

THE LEGEND IS BORN

In 1997, Che's body was found in Bolivia. DNA tests made a positive identification of the remains, and they were brought to Cuba for a proper burial. By that time, Che had long since become an icon of the Cuban Revolution and of the leftist movement in general.

Che had also become somewhat of a romantic figure for people—especially young people—around the world. These people weren't necessarily communists or socialists. For them,

Che's Famous Face

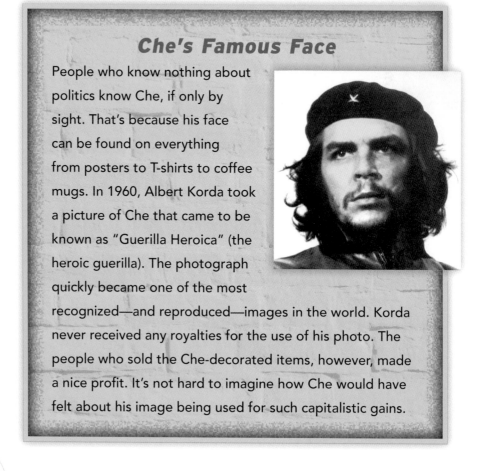

People who know nothing about politics know Che, if only by sight. That's because his face can be found on everything from posters to T-shirts to coffee mugs. In 1960, Albert Korda took a picture of Che that came to be known as "Guerilla Heroica" (the heroic guerilla). The photograph quickly became one of the most recognized—and reproduced—images in the world. Korda never received any royalties for the use of his photo. The people who sold the Che-decorated items, however, made a nice profit. It's not hard to imagine how Che would have felt about his image being used for such capitalistic gains.

Che's remains were returned to Cuba in 1997. Thirty years had passed since his death, but his legend remained as strong as ever.

Che represented a beautiful dream of equality and freedom from oppression for all. They focused on the notion that Che fought for the rights of the poor and downtrodden. They didn't necessarily think about the fact that Che used violent methods to attain his goals. Much controversy surrounds the legend of Che Guevara, but it has done little to diminish his heroic status. ❖

TIME LINE

1928 Ernesto "Che" Guevara is born in Rosario, Argentina, on May 14.

1930 Che contracts asthma.

1932 The Guevara family moves to Argentina's Cordoba province in the hopes that the mountain air will help Che's asthma.

1936-1939 The Spanish Civil War is fought.

1939 World War II begins on September 1.

1945 Argentina enters World War II on the Allied side; World War II ends on May 1945 (in Europe) and September 1945 (in the Pacific).

1947 Che's paternal grandmother dies; Che enters the University of Buenos Aires.

1950 Che travels through northern Argentina on a motorized bicycle.

1952 Alberto Granado and Che travel through much of South America.

1953 Che earns his medical degree in May and leaves Argentina for good soon after.

1954 The Guatemalan government is overthrown by a military coup while Che is living there.

1955 Fidel Castro and Che meet. Che joins the 26th of July Movement to overthrow the Batista government in Cuba. He marries Hilda Gadea.

1956 Che and Hilda's daughter, Hildita, is born. Che and other revolutionaries land in Cuba on December 2 for the start of the revolution.

1958 Che helps the revolutionaries win the Battle of Santa Clara, which opens the way for conquest of Havana, the capital city.

1959 Che enters Havana. Batista flees. The revolutionaries take over Cuba. Che divorces Hilda and marries Aleida March.

1960 Che's daughter Aleida is born. *Time* magazine features Che on its August 8 cover.

1961 The United States breaks off diplomatic relations with Cuba because President Eisenhower fears Cuba will become a communist regime. The battle of the Bay of Pigs is fought between American-backed Cuban exiles and Cuba. It ends in defeat for the United States.

1962 Che's son Camilo is born. The United States institutes a trade embargo against Cuba, no longer importing any goods (such as sugar) manufactured on the island nation. The United

States, Russia, and Cuba get into a deadly contest of wills when Russia places missiles on Cuba. The Cuban Missile Crisis ends when Russia withdraws its missiles.

1963   Celia, Che's daughter, is born.

1965   Che's son Ernesto is born. Che goes to the Congo to create a communist revolution there. He fails.

1966   Che returns to Cuba and soon leaves for Bolivia. He hopes to create a communist revolution in Bolivia and then carry the movement to his Argentine homeland.

1967   Che is killed in Bolivia by that country's military, who are assisted by the CIA.

1997   Che's remains are returned to Cuba and a funeral is held in Havana for the fallen revolutionary.

2004   *The Motorcycle Diaries,* the movie based on Che's travels through South America, appears in theaters.

2008   Fidel Castro retires as president of Cuba in February. His brother Raúl is elected president that same month.

A CONVERSATION WITH
Tom Hayden

 *Tom Hayden is a political activist known for his civil rights and antiwar work during the 1960s. In 1960, he founded the Students for a Democratic Society (SDS). He became a representative in the California legislature in 1982.*

Q. As a participant in 1960s politics, do you see Che as typical of revolutionary leaders of that decade?

A. Che, and those who overthrew Batista, were unique in their vision, physical courage, and organizational determination.

Q. As the decade progressed, did your feelings about Che, or the Cuban Revolution, change?

A. I was trying to concentrate on changing racism and poverty in America, but was aware that the Cubans were part of a Third World bloc that was similar in the sense of trying to break out of the Cold War Soviet–American mold. It was unprovable, but I always thought that U.S. acceptance of the Cuban Revolution would have allowed the Cubans to develop independently of the Soviet Union.

Q. What are your thoughts about Che's death?

A. [It] was an act of martyrdom on a global scale. I happened to meet with Fidel Castro … not long after Che's death, and I sensed the national sadness. Turning Che into a global symbol came with the loss of much analysis of why and how he died.

Q. At the time, did you think the communist government of Cuba, which Che helped establish, would survive as long as it has?

A. Yes, I never doubted that. While most Cubans want democratic and market reforms, they are not prepared to hand their island back to the United States. I have been to Che's memorial grave in Santa Clara, and found it very touching. I think he has been elevated to the status of a "brother" to all Cubans, rather than a political figure.

Q. Che would have turned 80 in 2008. Had he lived, and had he remained a part of the Cuban government, how do you think we might think of him today?

A. I think he would be proud of how many millions of Latin Americans and Central Americans ultimately followed his call to take up arms, how dictatorships gradually fell across Latin America in later decades, and how many of those former revolutionaries have become reformers in power, still trying to fight poverty, underdevelopment, and dependence on the U.S. superpower. I think he would identify with the millions of Latino immigrants who are remaking the culture and politics of this country.

Perhaps he would have inaugurated a version of Doctors Without Borders to deliver prenatal and preventive medical care to relieve the suffering of Latin American children. But I don't really know how he would have coped with his restlessness. He truly found extreme injustices to be intolerable in the depths of his being, and had no patience for patience.

Q. Che's image has sold more T-shirts than, possibly, any symbol in history. Why do you think this might be?

A. First of all, it's a great picture. The eyes are transcendent, gazing into the future. The beard signifies an independence. The photo made him a generic symbol of the beauty of rebellion. It also represents the infinite power of consumer capitalism, promoting image over substance.

GLOSSARY

Allied Powers: about 50 countries that fought Germany, Italy, and Japan during World War II

bazooka: an artillery piece meant to launch a projectile

beret: a type of hat, often worn in France, popularized in the United States by the Cuban Revolution

blockade: surrounding something, such as a coast, to prevent ships or troops from entering or leaving

capitalist: one who employs capital, meaning the tools and means of production, to make money and believes in private or corporate ownership

chauvinistic: showing excessive loyalty to one's gender to the detriment of the other

communist: one who believes in the communistic principle that wealth must be shared

conquistador: Spanish conquerors in the 16th century

coup: sudden overthrow of leadership

dictator: a ruler who has total control over his subjects

diplomat: someone who represents his or her country to other governments

exile: enforced removal from one's own land

exploitation: using someone or someone's possessions for one's self

fatigues: army clothing, often in dull colors

guerilla: someone who engages in irregular warfare

Hansen's disease: a skin disease, once called leprosy

heterogeneous: diverse; varied

incorruptible: incapable of acting falsely

indigenous: born in a land or region

insurgent: one who rises in active revolt

martyrdom: giving one's life for a cause

nationalize: to bring under state ownership

Nazi: a follower of Adolph Hitler in the 1930s and 1940s

neutrality: refusal to take part in a war between other powers

oppressed: pressed down or weighed down

proletariat: the lowest class of any society

propaganda: using slanted information to persuade

regime: a government, usually in a negative sense

revolutionary: one who seeks to overthrow a government

skirmish: irregular engagement between two small bodies of troops

socialist: a person who believes that the needs of society come before those of the individual

triumvirate: a group of three in joint control

tyranny: a government with an absolute ruler

vengeance: the act of taking revenge

FOR MORE INFORMATION

BOOKS AND OTHER RESOURCES

Deutschmann, David, ed. *Che Guevara and the Cuban Revolution: Writings and Speeches of Ernesto Che Guevara.* Sydney, Australia: Pathfinder, 1987.

Granado, Alberto. *Traveling with Che Guevara: The Making of a Revolutionary,* translated by Lucia Alvarez de Toledo. New York: Newmarket Press, 2004.

Guevara, Che. *Reminiscences of the Cuban Revolutionary War,* translated by Victoria Ortiz. New York: Monthly Review Press, 1968.

Lynch, Ernesto Guevara. *The Young Che: Memories of Che Guevara,* translated by Lucia Alvarez de Toledo. London: Vintage Books, 2007.

WEB SITES

Che Lives

www.che-lives.com
This web site includes a wealth of information about Che, as well as some of his own writings. It also features a gallery of rare photos.

Time 100: Che Guevara

www.time.com/time/time100/heroes/profile/guevara01.html
Discover what it was about Che that inspired *Time* magazine to name him one of the century's greatest "Heroes & Icons."

Publisher's Note: Our editors have carefully reviewed these recommended web sites, but we cannot guarantee that a site's future contents will continue to meet our high standards of quality and educational value. The publisher does not have any control over and does not assume any responsibility for third-party web sites.

SELECT BIBLIOGRAPHY AND SOURCE NOTES

Anderson, Jon Lee. *Che Guevara: A Revolutionary Life*. N.Y.: Grove Press, 1997.

Castro, Fidel, and Ignacio Ramonet. *Fidel Castro: My Life: A Spoken Autobiography*. N.Y.: Scribner, 2006.

Deutschmann, David, ed., *Che Guevara and the Cuban Revolution: Writings and Speeches of Ernesto Che Guevara*. Sydney, Australia: Pathfinder, 1987.

Granado, Alberto. *Traveling with Che Guevara: The Making of a Revolutionary,* translated by Lucia Alvarez de Toledo. N.Y.: Newmarket Press, 2004.

Guevara, Che. *Reminiscences of the Cuban Revolutionary War,* translated by Victoria Ortiz. N.Y.: Monthly Review Press, 1968.

Lynch, Ernesto Guevara. *The Young Che: Memories of Che Guevara,* translated by Lucia Alvarez de Toledo. London: Vintage Books, 2007.

Sandison, David. *Che Guevara*. N.Y.: St. Martin's Press, 1997.

PAGE 2

Sandison, David. *Che Guevara*. N.Y.: St. Martin's Press, 1997, p. 99

CHAPTER ONE

Page 9, line 23: Deutschmann, David, ed., *Che Guevara and the Cuban Revolution: Writings and Speeches of Ernesto Che Guevara*. Sydney, Australia: Pathfinder, 1987, pp. 330–331

Page 9, line 27: Ibid., p. 336

Page 10, line 7: "Bazooka Fired at U.N. as Cuban Speaks," *The New York Times*, December 12, 1964, p. 1

CHAPTER 2

Page 15, line 7: Lynch, Ernesto Guevara. *The Young Che: Memories of Che Guevara,* translated by Lucia Alvarez de Toledo. London: Vintage Books, 2007, p. 139

Page 15, line 12: Ibid.

Page 16, line 14: Ibid., p. 98

Page 17, line 5: Ibid.

CHAPTER 3

Page 25, line 6: Anderson, Jon Lee. *Che Guevara: A Revolutionary Life*. N.Y.: Grove Press, 1997, p. 61

Page 26, line 22: Granado, Alberto. *Traveling with Che Guevara: The Making of a Revolutionary,* translated by Lucia Alvarez de Toledo. N.Y.: Newmarket Press, 2004, p. 15

Page 28, line 19: Granado, p. 94

Page 30, line 15: Ibid.

Page 30, line 21: Ibid.

Page 30, line 27: Anderson, pp. 77–78

CHAPTER 4

Page 38, line 3: Lynch, p. 182

Page 40, line 8: Ibid., p. 230

Page 43, line 10: Castro, Fidel, and Ignacio Ramonet. *Fidel Castro: My Life: A Spoken Autobiography*. N.Y.: Scribner, 2006, p. 173

CHAPTER 5

Page 46, line 6: Lynch, p. 282

CHAPTER 6

Page 55, line 10: Castro, p. 183
Page 56, line 4: Guevara, Che.
    *Reminiscences of the Cuban
    Revolutionary War,* translated
    by Victoria Ortiz. N.Y.: Monthly
    Review Press, 1968, p. 44
Page 57, line 5: Ibid.
Page 57, line 11: Ibid.
Page 57, line 19: Ibid., p. 45
Page 60, line 4: Castro, p. 191
Page 61, line 21: Guevara, p. 165

CHAPTER 7

Page 66, line 2: Anderson, p. 476
Page 71, line 19: "Castro's Brain,"
    Time magazine, August 8, 1960

CHAPTER 8

Page 81, sidebar: Anderson, p. 414
Page 84, line 7: Castro, p. 278
Page 84, line 17: *London Daily
    Worker,* November 1962
Page 85, line 15: Anderson, p. 719
Page 86, line 4: Sandison, p. 99

CHAPTER 9

Page 94, line 2: Anderson, p. 739
Page 94, line 20: "End of a Legend,"
    Time magazine, October 20, 1967,
    p. 27
Page 95, line 7: Castro, p. 25

INDEX

ABOUT THE AUTHOR

Samuel Willard Crompton teaches history at Westfield State College and Holyoke Community College, both in his native western Massachusetts. The author or editor of many books for teenagers and young adults, Sam is also a contributor to the *American National Biography*. Sam served an internship at the John F. Kennedy Library during his college years, an experience that helped open his eyes to the tumultuous times in which Che Guevara lived.

Picture Credits

Cover, p. 69, 96: Newscom; p. 2: Joseph Scherschel/Time & Life Pictures/Getty Images; p. 6, 62, 67: Associated Press; p. 11, 97: Joe Cavaretta/Associated Press; p. 12, 14, 17, 21, 56, 72, 98: © German Gallego, Digital Press/Newscom; p. 22: Canadian Press; p. 24: © Jim Sugar/Corbis; p. 27: Martin Bernetti/AFP/Getty Images; p. 31: Eitan Abramovich/AFP/Getty Images; p. 34: Andrew St. George/Associated Press; p. 37: Frank Scherschel/Time & Life Pictures/Getty Images; p. 40, 41: © Bettmann/Corbis; p. 44: photo by Enrique Meneses/Rex USA, Courtesy Everett Collection; p. 47, 87, 95: AFP/Getty Images; p. 48, 74, 80: Sven Creutzmann/Mambo Photography/Getty Images; p. 49, 54: Roger Viollet/Getty Images; p. 51: Rodrigo Arangua/AFP/Getty Images; p. 59: Fred Mayer/Getty Images; p. 60: Hulton Archive/Getty Images; p. 64, 76, 90, 92: Keystone/Eyedea/Everett Collection; p. 79, 82: Getty Images; p. 100: Time & Life Pictures/Getty Images; p. 101: Michael Buckner/Getty Images.